Roadside Poems
Travels With a Pilgrim

Floyd Brandt

Copyright © 2014 Floyd Brandt.

All rights reserved. No part of this book may be reproduced, stored, or transmitted by any means—whether auditory, graphic, mechanical, or electronic—without written permission of both publisher and author, except in the case of brief excerpts used in critical articles and reviews. Unauthorized reproduction of any part of this work is illegal and is punishable by law.

ISBN: 978-1-4834-1118-7 (sc)
ISBN: 978-1-4834-1119-4 (e)

Because of the dynamic nature of the Internet, any web addresses or links contained in this book may have changed since publication and may no longer be valid. The views expressed in this work are solely those of the author and do not necessarily reflect the views of the publisher, and the publisher hereby disclaims any responsibility for them.

Any people depicted in stock imagery provided by Thinkstock are models, and such images are being used for illustrative purposes only.
Certain stock imagery © Thinkstock.

Lulu Publishing Services rev. date: 5/28/2014

Dedication

To all the friends, family and strangers throughout the world who have supported, encouraged and talked with me.

Introduction

Roadsides mark the edge of a pilgrimage and its wanderings and hold the flotsam and the wonder of life, of the building up and the breaking down. There rests refuse and beauty, the past and the present, aspirations achieved and aspirations forsaken. Living is both road and roadside requiring seeing and turning and sometimes going back. Heroes go on paths bounded by roadsides and often return past the same roadsides to where they began and" know it for first time".

> *I am a part of all that I have met;*
> *Yet all experience is an arch wherethro'*
> *Gleams that untravell'd world whose margin fades*
> *For ever and forever when I move.*
>   Tennyson

The poems were gathered from those written during the fifty years following the assassination of John F. Kennedy. They are bits of travel on five continents, the joy of meaningful maturity for two children, the birth of two grandsons and the death of my wife. While they have no claim to worldly excellence, they can claim an effort to express the sincere emotions and imagining of a pilgrim seeking.

Table of Contents

- Introduction 2
- NOVEMBER 22, 1963 7
- ROADSIDE MORNING FLOWER 8
- WILL 9
- JOY 10
- EGLISE NOTRE DAME 11
- THE MOUSE AND THE SPEAR 12
- SARLAT 13
- PROVENCAL LUNCH 14
- PATTERNS 15
- 212 N. NELSON 16
- GARDNER 17
- HONEYMOON REDBUD 18
- AND YET ANOTHER ROOM 20
- BLOOMS 21
- LIGHT TOUCHED LEAVES 22
- DRIFTING 23
- QUESTIONS 24
- PLATO'S CAVE 25
- ADDICTION 26
- TAOS 27
- COLORADO CABIN PORCH 28
- NIGHT 29
- DAFFODILS 31
- RYAN 32
- PRESS CONFERENCE 33
- ST. FRANCIS FALL 34
- FOURTH OF JULY 1998 35

PATCHES	36
TIDE	37
BAYFIELD	38
DAD	39
WHEN EARTH'S LAST PICTURE IS PAINTED	40
THE THREADS OF ME	41
THOUGHTS	42
WALKING LONDON	43
APRIL MORNING	44
RAIN	45
ISLAND OAK	46
DEMONS OF THE DAWN	47
AWAKENING	48
50TH ANNIVERSARY	49
SEVENTY-FOUR YEARS	50
SCREECH OWL	51
ELEGY	52
ALL IS WELL	53
MEMORIES	54
THE CHILD WITHIN	55
SILENCE	56
MAKE YOUR BED	57
KIMBALL MUSEUM	58
MORNING WALK	59
PALAIS du PAPES	60
HEART'S DEEP CORE	61
ADVENT	62
MOVEMENT	63
ANCHOR	64
PRAIRIE STORM	65
DICK	66
MORNING WHISPERS	67

RAY	68
WALK THROUGH UNIVERSITY HALLS	70
WOOD TROLL	71
BRAHMS' "A GERMAN REQUIEM"	72
MEMORIAL DAY	74
SEED	75
COLORADO CABIN PORCH	76
MENDEL'S PEAS	78
SUNDAY IN MARYVONNE'S GARDEN	79
GENTLE	80
A DISTANT FLUTE	81
EASTER	82
ADDICTION	83
NOTES FROM AN ASTRONOMY LECTURE	84
ODE TO A BLADDER	86
IN PRAISE OF ANNIVERSARIES	87
A WARM DAY IN JULY	88
SHADE	89
PORCH	90
ORTHOPEDIST'S WAITING ROOM	91
WAITING	92
THRESHOLD SPRING	93
SOFTLY	94
CHILL	95
TRANSPARENCY	96
STUFF	97
ALGORITHM	98
"YES MOTHER"	99
GILDED AGE	100
NEW STONES	101
MARTINI EVENING	102
MARTIAN TV	103

TENDER	104
NOVEMBER 22, 2013	105

NOVEMBER 22, 1963

Youth, strength and courage rode the street that day.
Cheering hearts rode with him on a sad street
It was a warm day, a fall day, a sad day,
In a Texas city near where the West begins.

He rode a majestic car on a warming day,
Where the sun shown and the people waved.
A young man, a fair man tall with greatness.
Thrice tested, twice victorious, once dead.

He was there and he was happy – He was there and he was dead.
In the instant of glinting sunbeam, in the crack of death,
Cradled in loving hands he died, cradled in many hearts he lives
He died as rode a sun lit street on a warm day, a fall day.

He was a young man and a fair man touched with greatness .
It was a warm day, a fall day when he died so quickly.
His was not a simple life, not a rude life but a full life
Born to wealth, touched with greatness, touched with destiny.

There by an underpass, just off Main Street in the sunshine,
He died there in a Texas city near where the West begins.
Hear now the requiem roar of a giant plane's funeral dirge,
Echoing through a warm day's white clouds, in a fall sky.

Muffled drums muttering tear stained rolls,
Long lines of silent mourners form.
The clutching breaths of a sorrowing land.
Whisper low, whispers" Ask what you can do…

ROADSIDE MORNING FLOWER

Through blacken globs of glowering grime,
That by the roadside now recline.
A piece of asphalt raw and dank,
Flung there beside the roadway's flank.
Uncultured grime the cities plight,
There rests a bit of oily, dirty night.
But from its midst there grew a stem,
Catching mornings early dim,
Amidst a brightly glistening shower
A gift to all, a yellow flower.
With grace a dance, a song of glee,
While by the burdened masses flee.
Who fail to pause their maddened pace
To see the tiny flower's golden face.

From a crack in a large clump of asphalt which had broken off the side of the roadway there grew a single green stem topped by a single yellow flower. April 1988

WILL

Small sounds to listening ears impart,
A song to joyful waiting hearts.
Embrace the wonder of life anew.
Life is here where good abounds.
Feel the rhapsody of circling arms.
Small fingers reach for all the world,
And greet the day with bits of bright,
To thrill the hearts of those who reach to you.
So lift their dreams and touch tomorrow's hope.
Go forth this day in light to meet the world.
To smooth again our wrinkled dreams,
And weave the threads of tattered hopes,
With jeweled promises yet to be.

July 1986 Birth of a grandson.

JOY

When work is through and lights are dim,
Then know the joy of tasks complete.
And pedestaled there upon the yet to be.

Firmly take again the hand held tool,
And strike the yielding metal of the self.
Then dust away the splinters of a restless soul.

Reach for light beyond the shadowed wall,
To know this day creation's rising song,
And see again the joy brightness of the day.

EGLISE NOTRE DAME

Stone on stone rises to a dome above,
To gather voices of the circling dove.
A dome capped home for souls in quiet repose,
Gathers dying sighs of human woes.
Saintly prayers a sacred breeze adore,
Softens pains they know no more.
A smoldering flickering candle flame,
That dimly lights the hope and eases blame.
To sweep away the hearts long darken cry,
And whispers soft a thankful sigh,
A grace touched life that dwells in each,
Beyond the past and now in saintly reach.

Sitting alone in the Eglise Notre-Dame in Bordeaux, France

October 6, 1995

THE MOUSE AND THE SPEAR

A child sallies forth with sword and full armor
Adventure to find in the world of tomorrow.
The search for the demon in wondrous play,
With spear and great courage the dragon to slay.
Fire breathing its roars fills his heart with great fear,
So quickly he scampers to the top of his spear.
What came to the mind as large as a house,
Now is no more than a soft tiny mouse.

So now we are armed with great shiny lances,
The dragons to slay in the world of romances.
With armor to hide so well our grim faces,
From demons who dwell in deep dark places.
The roar of our fears sends us climbing our spears,
To view with surprise the mouse that appears.

A small six inch pewter statue was purchased in Carcassonne, France as a gift for Stan and his family. This endearing statuette of a knight in armor who leaped out of his shoes to climb up his spear to escape from a mouse captured my fancy.

SARLAT

Ochre crowded walls that hide the past.
Hidden walls sustained the endless wars.
Rough walls to hide the bloody streets,
A tithe to sacramental mindless strife.
Fear and death beyond the walls,
Pain and sickness roamed within.
Choking fear dimmed mind and dreams.
Harsh ageless fears built monuments.
Remains of glittering treasures sought.
Rooms hide quaking hearts and fading dreams,
Raised beastly images but not the grace within.
The distant saber's striking sound.
Armor's fading, rattling refrain.
A breeze sweeps o'er the dank refuse,
Awaits tomorrow's morning light.

Oct. 9, 1995 while having coffee in the square of Sarlat, a walled medieval city in Southern France.

PROVENCAL LUNCH

A bee came to lunch in Aix-en-Provence,
To join with the people his response,
To words of great hope and gathering trouble.
To see what was there on a table so jumbled.
He flew through the sun in Provencal splendor
Past bright flowers their nectar to render,
To savor bright cloths which covered the table.
Then seek out the hostess' work so able,
Set jabon a' cru, bright wine and green salad.
Talk of far places and yesterday's actions
Of plans of peace to ease warring factions.
Then flee in alarm to join other bees,
Return to the smells of a platter of cheese,
Then fly all around and join the endeavor,
To relish the humor, so very clever,
Then rising up high above the great treasure
To join in the murmur of friendship's pleasure.

On October 14, 1995 there were seven of us having a marvelous Provencal lunch on the patio of Maurice and Maryvonne's country home in Puyricard, France a small village near Aix-en-Provence. It was a beautiful sunlight day, a Provencal day of exquisite beauty blending the soft blues of the sky with the fall warmth of the sun in Maryvonne's flower garden.

It the midst of all the conversation a bee suddenly appeared at the table and seemed to be enjoying the gathering as much as anyone. He flew from one person to the next and from one dish to the next for several minutes.

PATTERNS

Patterns cross the woven floor,
That feel the pace of endless search.
Shadows dance within the space,
Small flecks of now drop here and there.
Feels hastes' impetuous noisy throb,
Then awaits the soothing quiet of evening.

December 1995

212 N. NELSON

Crumbling walls mark each passing sigh,
Remembering now the tear dimmed eye.
The gleeful sounds of children's play,
Quiet echoes that mark a bygone day.

Hear again the hammers building,
The swirling sounds of children scrambling.
Then youth strides out past all the aging,
Past rows of eaves so slowly sagging.

December 2005

GARDNER

There midst storms that shake,
The broken stems of garden's blooms.
The ceaseless challenge of an endless season,
Touch plants with rays of youthful spring,
Then share the coolness of an autumn's time.
A canopy to shade against the summers heat,
A kindling cover against the wintry gusts,
Skillful weeding with experience, sharpened tools,
Receive the gentle rains that nourish budding life.
Hope's urges rising in seedling's bloom,
To welcome once again a gardener's touch.

1996

HONEYMOON REDBUD

When mother and dad were married in Yukon, Oklahoma in 1929, there was no money for a honeymoon so Grandmother and Granddad's farmhouse became their honeymoon cottage. The following morning they went for a walk along a small creek near the farm. There they spied a Redbud seedling about a foot tall which dad dug up, wrapped it in a handkerchief and carried it back to the farmhouse. They planted the seedling on the south side of the house and there it grew through the years to provide summer shade for me and my teenage uncle. It was a large tree twenty-five years later when my grandparents left the farm and moved to town.

In 1964, our first house in Austin had a large beautiful redbud growing in the back yard much like the one that is still standing next to that little farm house outside of Yukon, Oklahoma.

In 1974 we moved into a house on Redbud Trail in Westlake Hills across the river from Austin. Often before my early morning walks, I would fill my pockets with redbud seedpods which I scattered as I walked along the road. During our twenty two years there, numerous redbud trees sprouted among the road; spiritual offspring of the honeymoon redbud planted decades earlier by my newly married parents.

REDBUD HONEYMOON

A morning walk along a twisted lane,
Two lives now joined as one refrain.
And as they walked this first bright morn,
They whispered dreams so newly born,
Then there beside the trail a seedling small,
With heart shaped leaves, a lover's call,
That reached from soil to sunlit sky,
To welcome all who passed it by.
With loving hands they loosened soil,
And lifted it with gentle toil.
Then wrapped the roots with handkerchief,
And covered o'er each tiny leaf
Beside the aging house they placed the shoot,
And gently pressed the soil around each root.
To burst with spring's deep reddening bloom,
Beside the aging women's room.
Each passing year its bursting flower,
Announces spring and welcome shower.
To spread its canopy of cooling shade,
For those who followed from the glade.
And then another redbud's welcome bloom,
To shade the children's children from the noon.
For decades now the flowering tree,
Has sheltered all as season's flee.
Another redbud placed with care,
Beside a house a passing thoroughfare,
Adorned with redbuds Oh so frail,
Along a street named Redbud Trail.
Small children in its shade do play,
And hear the whispers of a distant day.
Watch the rose like buds emerge,
With every season's rolling surge.
The morning's walk down Redbud Trail,
Past cluster trees beside the vale.
Beside the trail there waits for me,
A flair of red tinged blooms, a redbud tree.

YET ANOTHER ROOM

So sweep away the waking gloom,
Then open doors to see another room.
Walk through its portals yet to see
That night has left its urge to flee.
Sing now a song that rolls beyond your lips.
Like billowing sail drawn bounding ships,
That leap to meet the morning sun,
And signal loud the day has now begun.

January 1, 1997

BLOOMS

Illumine now that weary fear swept soul,
Who stumbles midst the looming dark.
Where anxious gathering shadows roll
Cleanse grime from soul's dark mark.
Enter now faith's streaming light,
Embrace the mordant seeds unborn.
Then loose the bounds of sickly night,
'Til blooms spring forth to now adorn.

Aug 1, 2013

LIGHT TOUCHED LEAVES

Light seeps in across the sill,
And brushes out awakenings chill.
Bids me awhile in warmth to stay
Casts light to see the shadows play.
Rumblings from my mind depart,
And urges now my beating heart.
Moving time stands in patient awe,
To see the day's wind blown straw.
Rustling, dancing dew laced leaves,
In graceful patterns the sun receives,
.

DRIFTING

The views of me are not from me,
But stranded in the leaves that fall.
The eyes that see my eyes,
Stand out there beyond the me.

Tremors wake the drifting mind,
And wonder whence it comes.
Then turn to seek the trail it lost,
To drift again beyond the time.

The light I see comes in from there,
To brighten me from shadows cast.
And blinks from light to dark and back again,
Twixt rippling shadows slashed by light.

To hear with ears beyond my ears,
The pulsing hammers trip the sound.
The quivering strings respond,
With sound that whispers to the quiet.

I am there and I am here.
Like clouds between the peaks and vales,
Changing scenes bespeak tomorrow,
Then leave and travel there again.

QUESTIONS

There is a crevice deep before we sleep,
From which to view the questions stark.
To choose again how shall we live?
An endless search through waning years.
Shuffling steps within a breathless state,
Come oft this road, this dauntless trail,
To ask again the reasons old,
Of faith and hope of life itself.
And in our darkening days and gathering nights,
What lights to guide our souls to rest and peace?

PLATO'S CAVE

Tumult stirs the darkened thoughts,
That wander through this shadowed night.
Scrambled threads enshroud the din,
Where dwell the demons of the night.
Their shrouds are naught but flimsy dreams,
From whence they leap with shrieks of fear,
Escape their bounds and chase the light,
From endless caverns deep within.
Where nurtured shadows weave a web,
And out again they cross the mind,
Awakened souls then start to flee,
To find a place from which to see,
The demons falter then wailing flee,
In hide again behind that shadowed wall.

March 1997

ADDICTION

Like a flame the moth cannot deny,
The flickering light that beckons
To the cave that is not you.
Then sings to you a siren numbing cry.

A light approaches from afar,
Chases shadows from the cave.
Beckons you through all the dark,
Then lights the path to who you are.

TAOS

A table deftly set for bygone meals.

Hear the sounds of brushes stroking art,

And seek the morning's palette light.

And lifts the colors from an artist's grasp.

Flings dripping colors across the canvas bare,

Feel the brush stroke's in blended tones.

Gracious lives all wrapped in frames.

And softly brushes out the wrinkled days.

At a museum in Taos, New Mexico, the home built by the Russian artist Nicolai Fechin in 1927.

COLORADO CABIN PORCH

Quiet sentinels stand in stately groves,
Reach for the morning's opening light.
First rising pink then warming golden sun,
Soft nestled clouds round yonder rising peak.
Then through the meadow elk in droves,
Assail the greening shrubs and aspen bark.
The freshets from the rocks begin their run.
And in the hills the black draped raven speaks.
Quietness ebbs across each spreading vale,
As life begins to push from rock and glen.
Morning's doe treads quietly down the trail,
And nibbles newness from the spring again.

July 25, 1997

NIGHT

Night erupts in shadowed swirling streams.

Darkens all of terror's silence.

A pounding, pulsing heart,

Within the shivers of the night.

Thoughts fly out and back again,

Chasing dreamless dreams.

Then flees to distant corners of the night,

Where sleep awaits the morning's rays,

To light the day before another night.

NORMA

December 5, 1997 Anniversary

Many flowers have you brought to me
The riches of a nurtured loving garden.
Two score and four the years passed by,
The sun, the showers, the days, the nights.
Each flower's caress a simple kiss,
Circles round with flowing grace,
To yet another seed, another day,
To bloom again, to touch with light,
The waiting eddies of my heart.

DAFFODILS

Bright daffodils outside my pane,
Smile brightly from their peaceful place.
And sing their joys along the lane,
With softly nodding yellow blooms.
And bow again in hallowed prayer,
In joyful praise, to God's delight.
Where beauty sings on love's soft air.
The joy of now, in blossoms bright.

March 20, 1998

RYAN

In cradled arms where love resides
Where breathes the joy of newness found,
Tiny finger's softly grasp each loving heart.
See the glowing promises of peaceful sleep.
Radiance shines from sleeping eyes,
To light the wondrous task begun,
And see tomorrow's star entrapped.
Dream the dreams of life's beginning tasks,
 Prayers arise to meet tomorrow's sun.
Hear now the whispered songs he sings,
And hear the swirling hymn of all before,
The cadenced step from here and on beyond.
The tiny hero's quest for days unknown,
Goes forth from here in measured steps,
Returns to know its newness once again.

November 1996 A grandson

PRESS CONFERENCE

In wild abandon words come forth,
Paragraphing fizzles in the air.
One on top the other's thunder roll,
Authority speaks and freedom's sounds respond,
And form a line to reach for power,
Then tumble round colliding thoughts.
A hoard of wriggling words appear,
Collide and chase each other off the stage,
While meaning struggles from the floor.
Some flee to smaller rooms where gossip dwells,
Then leap through truth's bright window pane,
To trip on doubt's firm window sill,
And fall to miry pits below.
Then scrambling forth with words anew,
To seek another stage beyond the pit.

ST. FRANCIS FALL

St. Francis stands midst the flitting birds.
Flowers festooned around with summer's green.
Birds fly to sit upon his head then take the seeds,
He holds for them and smiles for me.

Near a wall that shapes the garden's edge,
Where sheltered vines their tendrils spread.
Birds fly with songs and colors bright.
Then down to rest and search for seeds.

St. Francis fell among the flowers,
Cradled head looked up with puzzled gaze.
The soften soil on which he stood
Gave way and flung him down.

What sermon preached while lying there?
Go find a firmer place on which to stand?
Shifting ground upsets a saintly stance?
Or, nature's sanctuary is not a place of rest?

A garden's quiet that soothes the mind,
Freshens spirits, buttresses the soul.
A place to stand before a flailing storm.
A place to rest, a place to fall.

FOURTH OF JULY 1998

Words marched past the aging souls,
Parading to the cadenced sounds,
Words that sing of freedom's dreams,
Words of yore engraved on hearts today.

Words that speak of timeless strength,
The girdle round the nation's varied all,
A day to share the names that span this land.

Huck Finn spoke of slave and free.
Pondered long the brotherhood of man.

Barbara Jordan's words and rolling tones,
A bell that tolls forth freedom's chords,

Daniel Webster's resounding sharpened words,
the powered words he heard when he was young.

Then words from Emerson, Fitzgerald and Frost,
Caressed the lingering image of this land.
To speak of strength and time and good,
And plead tomorrow's vision.

With stentorian tones a courtly judge,
Embraces law and speaks for truth, tells all,
Flags are not a cloth to hide our clutching views.

Lincoln smiles to hear Jake read his measured words.
Sam sighs to hear the wifely Abigal who wrote,
To urge Sam care for her and women evermore.
 Soft sound of shuffling chairs and lifted hearts.
Then an ice cream feast with berries red and blue.

PATCHES

"And no one puts a piece on unshrunk cloth on an old garment, for the patch tears away from the garment, and a worse tear is made." Matt. 9:16

The ragged soul that brambles tear,
Moves slowly through the passing day.
To seek another quick repair,
To cover yet another blemish on the way.
Toward the distant place beyond,
Moments quickened pace that seeks to know,
Whence from the tumbling hours respond,
Tis' time enough to catch the bending bough.
The tears and rends the soul's poor cloth,
With sighs from yet untraveled paths,
Go out to tend the rending sounds of life,
Where pleads the yearning soul's repair.

TIDE

Now breaks the swells of rolling tides,
To join the shores eternal moving flow.
Ripples count the passing hours,
Then flee beyond the rising shoals,
Hear yesterday's coursing waves,
Cast pluming doubts upon the beach.

Stand drenched before each passing gust,
And strain to see beyond the surf.
Go back a shrill small voice implores,
Go forth the challenged heart exclaims.
Turning back is not to know,
When time and tide will find an end.

July 1990

BAYFIELD

Walking down broad Bayfield streets,
Cadenced by the decades past.
Memories past from lips now sealed,
Whispered tales so oft now told.

Spreading limbs of aged trees,
Shadow's walk hides mind and will.
Then quietly pause to see past lives,
Retreat behind the dancing maple leaves.

Why here and not some other field,
To hear the sounds of yesteryear.
And fly beyond the oft pealed sounds,
Beyond the muted pulse of stifled breath.

With measured tread along the road,
I walk and think about this day,
Listen beyond today's soft sounds,
To yesteryear's quiet whispered echoes.

Hear now the straining soul's endeavor,
Stones piled on stones that built the wall,
That strained the limbs and stilled the pulse,
While countless days of rest stroll by.

DAD

During my childhood I shared many activities with my father, working together, fishing, Boy Scout camps, and then there were long days when he took me with him as he called on his customers – long days during which he drove hundreds of miles in the oil field, often on dirt roads. Those were the days when we talked and talked about many things, sometimes even about how far it was to the next grocery store where we could buy half pints of cold chocolate milk.

He had worked for a time as a sign painter and during much of his life he painted landscapes and an occasional still life or portrait. He was most happy when he was painting. He combined his painting and sign writing in a most curious way. He would find an abandoned roadside sign with the faded remnants of a tobacco ad, a patent medicine pitch or a Clabber Girl ad, then he would approach the rancher or farmer about repairing and using the sign. I do not remember him paying for the signs, they were just gifts from the landholder where they were located.

He would repair the signs, put a base coat of paint on them and then proceed to paint a landscape of lakes, pine trees and mountains or hills in the background. Certainly not Panhandle vistas, but images which I am sure sprang from his memories of the lakes and pines and hills where he grew up in Northern Michigan. Then he would tastefully letter *STANLEY W. BRANDT SUPPLY COMPANY* and his telephone number across the sign, careful not to interfere with the scenery.

I particularly remember one day when he was up on a stepladder painting one of the larger signs when I heard "*And they shall splash on a ten league canvas, with brushes of comet's hair.*"

A few months ago when I began memorizing various pieces of poetry, those few lines kept returning. I could remember the first line but I did not know the name of the poem or who wrote it. The internet supplied a lot of information about the poem written by Kipling. As I read the entire poem, memories filled my eyes. So now, each time that I recite it to myself, there is a certain polishing of so many memories and an image of golden chairs and saints and "things as they are."

WHEN EARTH'S LAST PICTURE IS PAINTED

Rudyard Kipling

When Earth's last picture is painted
And the tubes are twisted and dried
When the oldest colors have faded
And the youngest critic has died
We shall rest, and faith, we shall need it
Lie down for an aeon or two
'Till the Master of all good workmen
Shall put us to work anew
And those that were good shall be happy
They'll sit in a golden chair
They'll splash at a ten league canvas
With brushes of comet's hair
They'll find real saints to draw from
Magdalene, Peter, and Paul
They'll work for an age at a sitting
And never be tired at all.
And only the Master shall praise us.
And only the Master shall blame.
And no one will work for the money.
No one will work for the fame.
But each for the joy of the working,
And each, in his separate star,
Will draw the thing as he sees it.
For the God of things as they are!

THE THREADS OF ME

An ever present dream lies just beyond,

Where dwells tomorrow's threads?

In words that whisper oft to me,

Sometimes in children's churlish games.

Threads that weave the wisps of naught.

What seeks it now?

That waspish thread of me,

That ties the now to where I'll someday be.

May 22, 2000

THOUGHTS

The streaming yearning of the morn,
Grasp's my thoughts in silent ways,
Wrests me from night's quiet robes,
Thrust me once again into the day.

Thoughts that form my heart's reply,
In silence stroll a new found path,
Beyond the anxious striving noise,
To sweep away emerging sighs.

The foment of a surging life,
Moves past in endless tide,
Turns home again to evenings calm,
Then quietly dawns the robes of night.

WALKING LONDON

Age's shuffled tread down ancient ways,
Marked by years and signs of strain.
Tired limbs bear aching hearts,
Times remembered not forgot,
From past to now the quivering limbs,
When self is but a trailing strand.
A sprightly past a dimmed tomorrow.
Eyes that see through shadow's panes,
That blink away the aches, the pains,
Remember childhood's playful days,
Recall the fading wistful scenes.

APRIL MORNING

A brighter world enshrouds this day.
Clouds rise up in circling crowns
Leaves beckon and seem to say,
That joy is here so stop and see.

Then fades the day into the dusk.
And quietly draws the soft lit drapes.
Music wanes and fades the tune,
And leaves but echoes of a song.

How often is this scene replayed?
How shall the future days be told?
They come to me in bright array,
For spring illumines well this day.

April 20, 2002

RAIN

Soft rain falls slowly on my face,
in swathes that paint the day,
with misty drapes beyond the shore.
Palmetto fronds in graceful dance,
that grasp the rain in frightening gusts.
Round and round the whirling gulls,
before a plunge into the misty sea.
And from afar the rolling thunder sounds
above, beyond the light streaked sky.
Then lingers soft and whispers, Yes.

October 2004

ISLAND OAK

How wide the reach your oaken arms,
With many scars of ages past.
The twisting rage of fearful storms.
A thousand years have marked you well,
With fiery bolts and withering heat.
You stand with arms a shadow from the sun,
To shade a final age with tales to come.
So mark the follies and the times of trial,
Record the songs of winged flight,
Each spring's array of new born flowers,
Then grasp another star touched night.

October 2002

DEMONS OF THE DAWN

There is a snarl that wells within,
That spreads it stains and fears,
To every thought and fingertip.
It blankets prayers that strive to rise,
To lift and sing where silence lives.
An anger floods and grips the soul,
Where blame strides in and dims the light.
Tightness spreads through every breath,
And rancor slashes beauty from the eye.
Who shall I blame? Who shall I seek?
When tears release the demons of the dark,
That chase the dawn and on beyond.
Where is the light?
Its laughter and its ringing joy?
Each kindness held in mercy's grasp.
Shows gratitude's forgiving path.
Enfolds within soft comfort's care.
Undimmed eyes to see,
The beauty of this day.

AWAKENING

In stumbling jerks I see the world,
Through shadowed eyes I strive to see,
The reasons for my waking hour.
And peer through softened rising light,
The quivering thoughts that linger there.
Darkness poses scenes unknown,
Till light joins mind and lifts the soul.
Day breaks with soothing tones,
Life's tempo swells with passing steps,
And moves to garner all the light.
Bespeaks the life within the soul,
And pauses now in thankful sighs,
To hear the fleeing strains of night.

April 2003

50TH ANNIVERSARY

How short a time is fifty years,
Between the vows and this respite,
A few short trips 'twixt joy and fear,
Pilgrims on the path of life's delight.
Countless as the grains of sand,
The whispered words that softly say,
Take now and grasp my hand,
On this our anniversary day.

2003

SEVENTY-FOUR YEARS

The measured time of passing days,
Raced by with wild abandon.
What say I now as o'er them all,
The memories now to show the way.
To travel to this opening day,
What can I gather from this place.
The rolling tides of hours gone by,
Past craggy walls through meadows rare,
Through storms of sorrow, clouds of joy.
Down endless pilgrim paths,
To sprightly newness of each day.
Then move to catch the hope that dwells within.
To rest before the threatening clouds.
Bind lives to all that dwells within,
The songs of joy the chants of grief.
Till softly falls the final light,
Before the burst of rising peace

February 2004

SCREECH OWL

From morning streaks that end the night,
a mournful cry comes wafting from the dark.
Sharp sounds toward the breaking light,
And say to all who hear, I am no lark.
Or does it warn the shadows of the dawn,
To find elsewhere more frightening fare,
Then sounds again a screeching yawn,
From breaking dawn to darkened lair.

September 2005

ELEGY

Dear departed one,
Take this the mirror of my soul.
And in its mourning feel today,
Embraced by memory's ebbing flow.
Then tears flood eyes unused to flow,
'Till peace drops down,
Where silence dwells,
With tearful sighs that all is well.

July 2007

ALL IS WELL

How quiet the morn,
That whispers all is well.
Where rests the soul,
Beyond the fear and pain
And sings to me a quieting song,
That says again that all is well.
Where memories rushing stream,
Flows to join the rippling now.
How welcome is the soft beyond,
Where peace proclaims that all is well.
And bids us rest forever now,
To times eternal cadenced waltz.

July 2007

MEMORIES

Though you were mine,
Thee I did not own,
For you were free,
And not my own,
But only drifting memories.
Winged dreams of all that was,
dance to the heart and warm it now.
Soft touches felt, I could not keep,
dwell now in dreams that comfort me.
Soft whispers speak from out the past,
Caresses loving memories,
And sing a deep heart's love.

November 2007

THE CHILD WITHIN

Where childhood whispers softly dwell,
Amidst the scenes of yesteryear.
The tumbling play of manhood swells,
And sings of all that's yet to be.
The child within that calls to play,
That flees from song to tears,
And threads his way each passing day,
A knotted skein of whirling dreams.
His play abounds with memory's toys,
All scattered cross the passing years,
Between the tears beyond the joys,
He whirls in play through youth to me.
And when he's gone what shall I be?
Without the knotted threads of yore.
Shall I be only eulogy,
Or only child once more?

2007

SILENCE

Silence rises from the dark,
Drifts low below the clouds,
Then breaks amidst the song of trilling lark,
Then rests again on whispered breeze.
Silence rests beneath the stone,
Beside the soul's soft resting place.
It whispers low to you alone,
The song of times eternal pace.

MAKE YOUR BED

Morning's rays slip past the dark,

To open eyes that meet the light.

Rumpled sheets bespeak a restless sleep,

Record the rumpled days.

Smoothed sheets caress the breaking dawn,

Spread to catch the mornings rays,

To signal all this day is on its way.

A benediction following a prayer.

January 2008

KIMBALL MUSEUM

Finger's toil from bygone years,
To shape the scenes of faith and fear,
To carve the stone and etch the gold,
Unfold a story old and yet so new.
For heart and hearth the toil unfolds,
Did tears then feed the growing need?
Did sighs sound love or straining hands?
Who shall say when all's complete,
These images that cradle faith's relief.
Celestial scenes spring from brush's stroke.
How oft the saintly faces rise,
In countless forms in varied stone.
The hinge between the ancient and the new?
Bowed figures born of death and rising.
To worlds restored and life renewing

April 4, 2008

MORNING WALK

With thankful, thoughtful strides I walk,
The lightened sky foretells the rising sun,
Proclaims the day in lifting rays.
With meditative deepening breaths
Partake the morning's cool.
And feel the pulse of this another day.
Breezes nudge the leaves above,
To ease the dove's small smoothing coo,
Then joins the trills of mockingbird.
Traffic snarls are heard nearby,
The grinding of a gravel train,
Then drifts away beyond the grade.
The new day warms the soul,
As on I walk from here,
To where I'll be anon.

May 2008

PALAIS du PAPES

Stones on stones above a mitre cap

Rise high above the red red robes

Solemn chants adorn another flickering age.

Soft leather pads on smooth gray stones.

Echoes soft from darkened walls of yore,

The sounds of murmured sacred chants,

That come to rest within heart's repose.

In June 2008 during a visit to the Palace of the Popes in Avignon, France, after climbing endless staircases and then sitting on a stone bench overlooking a small grassy courtyard, my mind's ears and eyes began to imagine sounds and views

HEART'S DEEP CORE

Grief comes on softly lilting breeze,
From deep where dwells the evermore.
It rustles back behind the eyes,
To nudge the gently falling tears.
It catches breath in shortened gasps,
And binds the heart as though to say,
Another dwells within yet far away,
And weeps for that beyond the now.
There is a bridge beyond my view,
A glimpse of fancies stitched with dreams.
A cooling breeze brings yet a sigh,
From deep within and far away.
Whispers of love that never end,
Sing melodies often heard before.
Steals away to places yet unknown,
To join eternity's requiem.

ADVENT

May the beauty of this day,
Call you to a peaceful place,
Then quietly gaze upon the hill's,
Green robes of quietness.
The ancient sounds of hymns,
Caress memory's gentle thought,
Then circle round and round,
To reach beyond your prayers.
The day's light goes softly on before,
To guide the path of reverence,
A light before your steps,

May your angel of the morning wake you to the joy of each day.
May your angel of hope be in your spirit breathing in and out.
May the angel of your birth whisper to you in your living.
May the angel of your voice caress your lips with singing.
May your angel of presence walk with you through all the doors.
May your angel carry you gently to the earth when breath expires.

December 2008

MOVEMENT

So sing with eyes that flash with light,
The rolling sounds of gathering flight.
And wish away the clouds dark night,
And lift in loving arms an aching plight.

To gaze outside the darkening room,
Where day falls back from flight so soon.
Like creeping shadows on the moon,
Hear now the wail of mystic loons.

Whence comes the cry of inward child?
And deep the moans of life so wild.
Then comes relief, the soft the mild,
And pauses once again to rest awhile.

                                      May 1989

ANCHOR

A battered soul within the storm.
To and fro in stormy violent swings.
Anchored deep on promise's reef.
Through calm and storm the anchor holds,
Safe from grasping ragged cliffs beyond.
A captain guides the storm tossed soul,
Through waters deep beyond the shoals,
 Beyond the looming storms to quiet beyond.

PRAIRIE STORM

Small children playing in the street.
Teens walking, talking, dreaming,
Sick old in porch bound chairs,
Watch the drama on the street.

Listen to the rambling endless talk,
From deep within the quivering minds.
Fears arise from years' uncertainty,
Isolated in corridors of thought.

Eyes that strain beyond a clouded light,
Reach for shades taunt string,
And chuckle at the children's antics,
 Before the dark and gathering clouds.

Then Prairie's bounding tingling rain.
Fresh coolness, flashing thunder claps,
Applaud a gently falling summer rain,
That brings cool breeze's velvet hymn

February 1999

DICK

Hear echoes of boyhood shouts at play.

Youthful dream of ever greater heights,

To hike to yet a further hill.

To raise a tent another day,

Moon laced canvas house of dreams.

To laugh the sudden laugh and feel the joy.

Of circling hawk and passing birds.

To see in them the heights to reach,

To know each by color and by song,

Racing canoes to drifts of restfulness.

Talk to plumb the depths of this grand day,

Bathed in sounds of youthful words.

And hear once more the dove's soft song,

Than step toward the dawn of yet another day.

To grow the years and know what went that way.

Written on May 6, 1996 during the funeral of my friend Dick McCune who died after ten years in the Alzheimer's hospital in Kerrville. We were together in the Boy Scouts more than fifty years ago. He was talented, intelligent person who served as the outdoor editor for the Dallas Morning News and as editor of the Texas Parks and Wildlife magazine.

MORNING WHISPERS

The quietness of another day.

The softened life of newness threads the clouds,

Rustling clothes and morning sounds,

Rise up to join the mounting flow,

Of racing dreams and fears suppressed.

The day begins with sunlight's cadenced pulse,

Before the sounds drown out the peace.

RAY

Yon buoy swings round to face the tide,
a mooring strong to anchor there.
Lay too, swing round to ease the flow.
Hear well the bell that sounds for you.

Beyond the rising waves to buoys,
long waiting thee and all to come.
To join the rolling decks beyond,
To find the place of softening quiet.

The fierce long night has passed,
The storms their drench have ceased.
The winds subside to softening breeze
and soothe the flow to easy drift.

Then comes in time a whispered call.
Its lilting song drifts o'er the cove.
To anchor here and rest a while.
Life's tasks have ceased for now,

The moorings fast midst softening swells.
Your home is here midst drifting clouds.
Dusk yields to night's awakening light,
Then comes the dawn to open this another day

August19, 1995

This was written at Ray Sommerfeld's memorial service after he drowned in Lake Travis taking his grandson fishing on his sailboat. He was a friend and colleague for about 30 years and we often sailed together. We shared many good social and professional events including celebration of Barb and Ray's 25th anniversary atop the Sheraton Hotel in Singapore. He was the son of a Lutheran minister and always conducted his activities with dignity and integrity.

EAGLE CLIFF

Through dew touched grass we quickly stride,
And see the swallow's winged swept glide.
To feel the morning's warming beam,
And hear the soothing swirl of Cascade's stream.
Toward the mountain Eagle Cliff,
So tall before the clouds adrift.
Across the Thompson's rough hewn bridge,
To start the climb along the ridge.
With hiking sticks we start the climb,
Soon pounding hearts mark a steep incline.
We pause and watch a hawk's long upward wheeling,
And feel the sounds of labored breathing.
Then upward still along a rocky trail,
We rise above the green robed vale.
Of trees that hide the valley just below,
To free the mountain peaks in stately row.
Soon tiring legs and heaving breasts,
Demand we pause again for rest.
We sit while eyes drift up toward the sky,
Where soon we'll be where eagles fly.
Past single pines and over rocks we scramble,
Near fallen trees and lowly bramble.
Until at last we stand atop the granite rift,
And view with awe the world from Eagle Cliff.
Beauty spans the world below in awed refrain,
In spreading green across the soft moraine.
With sweeping threads of blue that gleam,
While tumbling down to join another stream.
They catch the melting snow from distant height,
To form the azure pools where birds alight.
And join the downward rushing streams that flee,
To clover fields where feeds the whirring honeybee.
Sit here above the noise below God's ceiling,
In silence gaze upon the world and on our being.

WALK THROUGH UNIVERSITY HALLS

Strange sounds inof busy empty halls,
Where now I walk again.
A life within this place was mine,
'Til years said walk another way.
Echoes softly tell of bygone tasks
Which wait the hands others toil.
Greet those who wait their turn,
Time's ceaseless urge to be another time.
How different is the sameness of this place.
Where restless youth abides,
Passing days sweep all beyond,
To yet another breaking day.
Do listen to the sounds that were
Hear the mounting sounds of now.
Where shall we rest midst passing time,
While tiredness views the anxious tide.
Feel regrets without a voice,
Then still the flow of fleeting days.
View the beams of sunsets yet to be.
See the near and yet so far.

WOOD TROLL

An aging oak's dark ragged bark

Catches morning's sprightly rays.

Then forms a jowled face beneath the limbs,

a sprightly troll is there,

for those who care to see.

On my walk, there is an oak tree with a strangely shaped knurled outcropping on its trunk. By morning light the bark and shadows form the image of a troll.

March 15, 1997

BRAHMS' "A GERMAN REQUIEM"

I

On singing winds my soul escapes.
Voices course throughout the night,
And wrap me in a softness of the new,
Rising sounds pour deep within my heart.
Then swells and lifts again to newer heights.
Ecstatic whirls rise to meet the light,
Whence comes my catching breath?
That lifts me high to touch again,
Tomorrow's chorus where life rebounds.
Trembles softly over the grief and tears,
Takes the soul and reaches out for life,
With angel wings that waft away the tears,
And gathers all with tight bound chords,
To feel the warmth of heaven.
Kindles glowing embers around the heart,
Sweeps all to warming clouds of beauty.

II

Pounding drums and fearful strings,
Covering clouds of massing sound,
In endless chords I hear them now.
Their ruffling shuffling cadence
Drawn from deep, deep within,
Then shrinks before the baton's stroke,
Or sings of hope before it's flight to,
Crescendos rising up to speak,
Of death and on beyond.
Lifts up the soul that knows,
In search of endless restless quiet.
Peace and hope that rise far beyond,
And drifts us to a settling peace.

III

Songs each tendril heart entwines,
When moments flee from sounds.
Who struck that chord that reaches me?
Sweeps away the tiredness of an endless day.
Caress with care each painful twinge.
The grasp of life sweeps past the ending throb.
Hearts from the centered heart of God,
March in swelling throngs to greet the song.
Promises of hope sustain ere life was formed,
To hear the endless sounds of joy,
That come to fill the anguished dark of night.
In rising plaintiff throbs come back again.

March 1997

MEMORIAL DAY

Pangs that rise from trumpet sounds,

Creep oe'r long rows of crosses in a field.

And whisper soft the cannon row,

Til quieting death drifts oer the whole.

Echoes of the muffled sobs from those who knew,

The lingering sighs of those who are.

Memorial Day in Santa Fe, New Mexico, May 1997

SEED

Seed words speak of growth to be,
Residing there in futures's womb.
Chanting prayer of vision's wonder.

Add to thoughts now forming,
Add to flowered dreams aborning,
To form tomorrow's greater dreams.

Swirling dreams rest so quietly,
Before they rise to heavens peaks,
Above the gently nestled seed

That sped across the days,
Resting in the graceful turns of earth,
To touch a small seed's earthly womb.

It is the throbbing yet to be,
That guides the quivering seed.
To be tomorrow's strongly rooted tree.

COLORADO CABIN PORCH

Quiet sentinels stand in stately groves,
Toward the sun, the winters gales.
Then through the meadow elk appear.
With careful pensive exploring steps,
The greening shrubs and aspen bark assail.
First rising pink the warming golden sun,
Soft nestled clouds round a rising peak.
The freshets from the rocks begin their run.
And in the hills the black draped raven speak.
Quietness ebbs across each spreading vale,
As life begins to push from rock and glen.
The morning's doe treads quietly down the trail.
And nibbles newness from the spring again.

July 25, 1997

HANDEL'S MESSIAH

Rolling, roiling spirit carried,
On sounds ethereal.
Lilting sounds that fill the ear,
Vibrate the heart,
And whirl around the earth,
To come and rest again inside.
The sound of grand amen.
Steps of heavenly dances,
To slow cadences of man's striving.
Midst people now seeking.
Comfort ye who are comfortless,
Breathe before you cry for comfort
Seek the sounds of majesty
Kneel before the voice
That prepares the way.
Walk with strength in paths forgiven
Through every valley of quietness,
Every vale of exaltation.
Walk in peace and greatness
O'er paths now made straight.
Feel the rumble in every limb,
Feel the cry of joy and fear.
The crooked made straight, the step sure.
Praise creator glory of all creation
Exalt all promises enraptured.
To hear the sounds.
The flowing lilting certain song
In clouds of rising, throbbing praise.

MENDEL'S PEAS

With pad and pen a cowled monk upon a graveled path,
A cloistered garden filled with twining peas.
He dusts the pods and softly picks a few,
Then notes the plant from whence they grew.
Opens pods to count and list the peas,
And gently lifts each one with care,
Chin upon his folded hand he whispers low,
Why, O Lord, are some so round, some so wrinkled too.
Unknown to him a secret hides within each pea,
In both the wrinkled and the rounded too.
A Nobelian double helix softly waits,
For future chins on hands to wonder, what is next.

February 2010

SUNDAY IN MARYVONNE'S GARDEN

Cathedral's growing spires reach high.
The sound of birds,
Rose choirs and lavender isles.
Soft sounds, soft sighs, soft tones.
A lily padded carpet's blooms profuse,
Stirring gently in the softening breeze.
Below the flashing fish,
Whose gold leaps up to sunlit rays,
A prayer, a meditation so profound,
Caresses lips a heart then rests.
Steps the smiles the lifting heart,
Of one whose touch was felt so oft.
Beyond the swaying trees of pine,
Drift clouds of dreams to come.

Notes from the Garden of Maryvonne Saias, in Puyricard, France on Sunday June 19th, five weeks after her death on May 10, 2010 while walking on a pilgrimage to Sandiego Compestelo, Spain.

GENTLE

Steps along a walk,
A bell, an open door.
A flashing sunlit smile,
A soft embrace a gentle kiss.
Hands clasped with singing hearts.
To gently hold another life renewed.
Time taught memories come tumbling forth,
While streams of thought flow from the past,
And then another soft embrace, another gentle kiss.

January 2011

A DISTANT FLUTE

Incline your ear toward the stars.
Then listen with an inward ear,
Hear the tumbling, trilling bars,
Gathered sounds from outer space.

Lonely breath filled notes go round,
To gather once again above the clouds,
A vast chamber for the sound,
To hear a flute from outer space.

Mozart lifts his eyes in quiet surprise.
Raises hands and softly touches keys.
Hears star touch rising rhythmic chords,
And dreams again of harp and flute.

Toscanini rises softly from his chair,
Lifts and gently raises hand on high,
With dreamlike heavenly care,
Directs the clouds to one more chorus.

And in her own small world above,
Clouds below and stars beyond,
She plays her flute, a sound of life,
For those endowed with ears to hear.

On learning that a friend astronaut Caty Coleman was playing her flute on the International Space Station.   February 10, 2011

EASTER

Gray clouds with misty trails,
Await to hide the rising sun.
The world with lifted eyes,
To welcome the awakening light.
Wait with awe a Son's uprising,
Mystic rising to songs of praise.
Centuries march in stolid cadence,
Down that anguish shrouded hill.
An image stark bears history's cry,
To hallow the day through time.
Promises sublime of joy unknown,
When earthly days shall end.
How shall we know the all,
That flows from deep to deep?
Our "Whys" cling in trembling disarray,
Awaiting benediction's endless hymn.
Beckons faltering pilgrim's step.
To free the quivering all, that dwells within.

April 2011

ADDICTION

Like a flame the moth cannot deny,
A flickering light that beckons
To the cave that is not you.
Then sings a siren numbing cry.
Light approaches from afar,
Chases shadows from the cave.
Beckons you through all the dark,
Then lights the path to who you are.

May 2011

NOTES FROM AN ASTRONOMY LECTURE

Clouds collapse to smaller quarks,
Then fall away or fall without,
'Til beckoned by a hole of black.

Then piece by piece to bright lit stars,
Chase behind and round the moon,
To save each other from the other.

Fall into black holes again,
And. pound the clouds 'til nothings left
Blown hither, thither and to yon.

Jets of sun disrupt to narrow beams,
Shooting holes in clouds immense,
Then form a silicon cloud of dust.

A jet shoots out an awesome blast
Against a wayward star,
Then pauses for a while to wonder why.

Some away and some toward
The blank space twixt the stars
To wander someplace evermore.

Then screams through angular dimension
And spins away for years to come or go
A break from planets staid and quiet.

Another star shoots out again
And knows not where to go
Then collides and scatters all around.

Mock two a sounding shock.
Surprised to strike a floating star,
Then falls again into a hole of black.

Clumpy jets of fire loom up ahead
Then bang a cloud with wild abandon
Quickly leaping over slower clumps.

The universe swirls in wild array,
A thousand stars light another stellar blast,
To form another who knows what.

Carving holes holes incoming,
To birth again an unknown other,
While inner rings unstable race to outer rings.

Tiny crystals of stellar fragments reflect
The mess that fills the space,
Then fling them back to searching eyes.

Herschel looks at stars a forming,
Bright and flaring on they go
An outburst wild and still a coming.

Bright but fading time remains,
To find a place among the new
A hiding place to wait another cosmic blast.

Gas outflowing sweeps with fiery tails
A hundred years of light to free,
A bright and flaring star.

There is no night there is no day
Black holes and fiery mountains
To form a trembling universe forever.

ODE TO A BLADDER

A mighty chorus wells within
Where sounds again the measured voice,
In songs a bounding chanting chorus.
Le fois joins in and smooth's the strains,
While stomach sounds the base refrain,
Buried deep another organ's churbling chord,
Abruptly ends the moving rising inward sounds,
To seek again a resting room.

January 2011

IN PRAISE OF ANNIVERSARIES

Praise be for anniversaries,
For birthdays that mark the years,
For celebrations small and large.
For holidays that note the passing.
For days of saints that toll from belfries past.
For all beginning and the endings,
For books of past and future days,
For clocks that mark our waning lives,
To give us proof that we were here.

A WARM DAY IN JULY

It was eleven on Sunday morning a warm day in July.
It was a morning with sun and wreaths of sorrow.
Distant hymns echoed beneath a chapel spire,
It was a Sunday morning on a warm day in July.

A gasp, a quiver, a final breath
and stillness.
Life and spirit joined
that mysterious caravan.
Whispered prayers blessed a journey
just begun.

It was a Sunday morning on a warm day in July.
Bowed heads around a quietly resting form.
Shrouded tears and muffled sighs,
Farewell, goodbye and peace eternal.
It was a Sunday morning on a warm day in July

July 22, 2011

SHADE

How Cool a patch of shade,
But only for a while.
A measure of the sun lit hours,
It grows and moves and ebbs and flows,
Illusive as a shadow's waltz,
Following clouds it drifts before the sun,
Someplace here perhaps out there,
Or just behind a spreading tree.
Then flees the setting sun.
To evening's waning light,
To dream its nightly dream,
Of morning's early beams.

August 2011

PORCH

Listen to the creaking rockers,
Hear the aged talk the endless words,
From deep within their tiring hearts.
Joy and fears spring uncertain from the past,
Fulminations of a severed time,
Scattered minds upon a pilgrimage,
Hear softly spoken sounds.
Murmurs from deep within the soul.
Fading sounds so softly just beyond,
The sagging railings of the porch.

Children playing in the street.
The restless young on idle walks,
Talking, dreaming, yearning, passing by,
The old and sick sit staring from a porch.
A breeze before a highland rain.
Fresh coolness flows from thunder's clap,
Soft splashes of the summer rain,
That ease the glowering summer heat.
Dances with each splash of rain,
Sings with every rustling breeze,
With soft caresses to the skin,
A gift to people parched upon a thirsty land.

November 2011

ORTHOPEDIST'S WAITING ROOM

Quite murmurs midst the tattered magazines,
Patients sit before a gabbling staff,
Pain sneaks a view from eye lit caves,
While anxious eyes meet dull acceptance.

Sitting there amidst a growing nests of canes.
A name is called, a sudden start,
Shuffling slow toward the door,
Down halls to tiny rooms an antiseptic whiff.

From an ancient glass museum case,
Yesterday's instruments to cut and stretch,
To show how limbs were changed,
A shivering display of pain.

Sit in blank and shuffling quiet,
Hear faintly scratching pens,
Upon the endless paper forms,
That flow to ever growing files.

Time squats within a waiting room.
Why are doctors always late?
Is it because they schedule wrong,
Or wait your warranty's ending date?

September 2011

WAITING

With whiffs of medicine smells,
I sit and wait the calling of my name.
Like swirls of Autumn's rustling leaves.
Voices trickle through the walls,
To anxious ears and placid waiting.
Then a call to come and wait again.
Amongst dissection charts on every wall
Then like a huge white bird he comes.
To peer at you and how you feel.
Questions fly like driven leaves,
A dance of words, a waltz of wills.
Splendid confusion abounds in wonder,
While chilling stethoscopes pose,
An entitlement of unasked questions,
Trapped by whirling embellishments.
Precursors of the yet to be, then,
Flees to a darkened recess behind the eyes.
Resolution strides in with tightened jaw.
Acceptance seeks a shelter in the soul,
And begins the search for rest and quiet.

December 2011

THRESHOLD SPRING

Winter's somber frigid grasp.
Bleakness shivers in its storm,
Of winter's guard against a season's end.
Holds for now the restless surge of seeds,
And spring's harmonic sprightly voice.
The ageless urge of spring aborning,
Welcome newness brightly colored,
To light the path of winter's timeless trek.
Spring garbed in unawareness,
Joins the march of changing seasons.
A pirouette of ageless change,
Then awesomely, it's everywhere.

March 2011

SOFTLY

I sit and weep for what?
For all the years till now?
For marks upon a standing stone.
My mark upon that stone?
Hear   chimes with soften tones,
Feel the breeze caress the years,
Soft sound that soothes the deep within,
Softens all the past, tomorrow too.

CHILL

Where went thou fragile warmth,
In yesterday's shawl so softly knit,
From past yarns of many colors
Drawn from skeins of "all is well."
To form a shawl that warms the soul,
Warmth against the winds cold chill,

Must I each day knit yet another scarf,
To warm again a chill touched soul.
Yesterday's warmed my soul right well,
The chill today comes yet another way.
Yesterday's shawl has lost its glow,
I dare not fail to gather threads anew,
To weave another fabric for this day,

Threads of hope so softly drawn,
From memory's silver strands,
To form anew a fabric's weave,
The warmness of another shawl today.

December 2011

TRANSPARENCY

From rapt attention's row on row,
Screaming queries fill the nervous air,
Pulsing hands are raised on high,
Grasping for a fleeting grand illusion.
To seek a look beyond the fence,
For reasons oft opaque?
To see the rascals run from light?
Or see a glass walled show?
Its them not us who pulled the shade,
To hide what's surely there to see.
To leave imagination's themes,
And peer behind the rustling veil.
Jumbled questions rise from deep within,
Along the path of massive nodding votes,
Let every one step through to view,
Darkened shadows on yet another wall.

May 2013

STUFF

Fresh coffee smells embraces all.
See the sunlit rows of plants.
Some graceful, others wilting,
Begging for a hose or digging prong

Then to the garage to search O my,
Behind the other car below a dusty bike,
There's the lamp I lost another year,
What was   I was searching for?

The chill requires a sweater's warmth,
Where in this closet is the gray.
Hid among the closed packed rows,
Hanging there in wrinkled disarray.

Where is the cell that rings and rings,
A neighbor seeks that promised book.
Is it somewhere among the stacks,
Of books and papers all disheveled?

Stuff is where I live in great abundance,
It fills the house, garage and me.
How precious is that soapstone statue,
Bought in Africa, I think.

I'll go to mix myself a drink,
Relax and cool my fevered brow.
Which of fourteen half filled flasks,
And seven shakers hiding there?

June 2013

ALGORITHM

A step-by-step procedure used in calculation, data processing, and automated reasoning.

A number stands beside another.
Dashes down the data hall to seek,
A partner odd or even and join parenthesis.
Then from a file it plucks a power ,
Then greater speed down yet another hall,
Through files of facts from yesterday,
Then pause to gaze again,
Upon the languid damsel, hypothesis,
Reclining midst the blooming questions.
Then dashes up projection stairs,
Stumbles at the top on yet another multiplier,
Checks for bugs within a gaudy flowing chart,
Then down a corridor filled with powered digits ,
Careens around unexpected glitchs,
And stumbles through solution's door,
Then collapse on reason's couch to wait some more.

May 2013

"YES MOTHER"

No dinner gong, a whistle of the train.
A dining car's, panoramic moving scene,
Through windows stained by yesterday,
Cadenced by clicking, rolling wheels of steel.

Four dinner guests assigned a rolling table,
Faltering words of greeting parsed awhile,
Swaying guests arrive at other tables.
Then talk begins in faltering phrases.

Where are you going?
Where have you been?
And then an aging mother speaks,
Stammering confusion, a daughter's sigh

When will we see Clara? she asks.
Her aging daughter frowns, "Yes, mother,
Clara's is where we've been.
Clara was so glad you came."
Again another silent sigh.

"Daddy works so hard. Why aren't we home?
"I need to fix his breakfast. He can't do it alone."
"Yes, mother." A whispered, "He's been gone for years."
"I don't like where I live. We should take the kids, back,"
"We should go back to the house that Grandpa built."
"Yes, mother, as soon as we get home.
"We're almost home, let' go back to our seats."
"Yes, mother, as soon as you finish your breakfast."

August 2013

GILDED AGE

Echoes from a gilded past,
Set in stone on rising stone,
Resting there to serve a gilded age,
With stately measured steps.

Velvet scrolls and ancient art,
To cover walls beyond more walls.
Encased in marbled robes,
Within a green swept garden gown.

Shining coaches and prancing horses
Hear the jingle of the coaches,
Harness polished to shining brightness.
Regel dress bows steps down with care,

Music fills the evening air.
Gowns swirl in graceful rounds.
Livered servants to their coves repair,
To stand as breathing statues there

Waltzes whirl in measured moves,
All jewels beneath the glittering lights,
Dances filled with billowing gowns,
Formed in music's dancing squares.

October 2013

In the garden of the Mansion "Elms" in Newport, Rhode Island

NEW STONES

New stones appear beside the old.
Names etched in grays and tans.
Standing stones that mark the yester years
Tell the days of then and now,
With row on row of granite stone.
Silent sentinels to mark the past,
When love and laughter dwelled.
Stepping stones from that below,
To hearts and skies above.
Silent music joins with earthly sounds,
To seek life's mystery once again

October 2013

MARTINI EVENING

Long hours of mindful endless screens,
Tired words pirouette from dancing keys.
A soft seductive sofa beckons come sit,
To ease this ceaseless streaming life.

Then hear the rattle of the ice,
Reach down, stab an olive like a foe,
Hear it splash amidst the icy floes,
Then feel the coolness of the glass.

A sigh to ease the settling flesh,
Begin the evening sips of ease.
Smile as pundits spin their tales,
Softened by my olive chase.

Liquid joins with ice to weave,
A pleasant time of soothing quiet,
Gathers evening's tempered smiles,
Foretells the restful reading hours.

November 2013

MARTIAN TV

Hovering twixt a landing and the earth,
My screen records a picture of below.
Short dramas staged between the boredom.
A magic potion named Cialis teaches,
How to smile and show affection for each other.
Prepares them for a place called Sandals,
Where all turn young and sparsely clad,
Running to beaches, drinking places and oft to bed.
Strange animals that talk to startled humans.
A green lizard in a strange but different voice,
Who walks on hind legs and talks incessantly,
A white duck with a one word to speak,
Seems to joke at human foibles.
Huge animals with two tails and very large ears,
Sit on people to help their breathing,
Or follow close like mammoth sentries.

Some people go from youth to age in only seconds,
A tree falls in the forest screams "Look Out,"
Sleek wheeled vehicles with unseen horses.
Monsters flash or fly with tails and ugly faces.
Pills for indigestion, congestion and constipation.
Creatures tightly wrapped with bulging rounded fronts,
Join electronically with larger bearded wonders.
Two small groups each dressed in different colors,
Face an oblong ball then charge and strike each other.
Possessions are given but always called a "Sale"
Tis a strange and frightening sphere this Earth.
My Martian training tells me I have learned enough,
So power up and off I go back to the certain.
Free of talking animals and little pills.

TENDER

A bridge builder, a pontifect
International strand of cable.
Shore to shore and soul to soul.
Cables linked from you to me.
Tower to tower flings the words
An endlessly flow of this and that
Airwaves sweep from there to here
Ancient signals smoke upon the hill
Small lights flicker with a code
Wires span deserts click by click
And tenders move from ship to shore.

October 2013

NOVEMBER 22, 2013

On the 50th Anniversary of John Kennedy's Death

Memories of a sunny street out where the west begins,
Memories from a muffled drum parade,
A simple bugle echoing hill where silence dwells
Around a simple gas lit grave.
The face the words live on amidst the strife.
The striving and the angst live on,
Outside the quiet resting upon upon a hill.
Far from that sun drenched western street.
The dreams he dreamed, the path he strode,
A faded breathing gasping bit of history.
No more the tears the choking breath
Who watched the flag draped caisson past.

So many promises echoing strong, yet hearing still,
The young man, the strong man who rests upon the hill,
Ask not…………

Milton Keynes UK
Ingram Content Group UK Ltd.
UKHW010026040324
438776UK00002B/439